AR

# The SPX 2004 Anthology
Published by the Comic Book Legal Defense Fund

Edited by Greg Bennett, Charles Brownstein, & Chris Pitzer

Front Cover art by Steve Lieber - www.unrewarding.com/steve
Back Cover art by Zack Soto - www.studygroup12.com
Ink Bottle art by Joel Priddy - www.pulpatoon.com

Produced by The Expo to benefit the Comic Book Legal Defense Fund.

Expo 2004. All rights reserved. All comics stories ©2004 by their respective creators.

Design/Production: Chris Pitzer, pitzer@adhousebooks.com
Thanks to John Gallagher.

No part of this book (except small portions for review purposes) may be used without expressed written consent from the CBLDF.

ISBN 0-9721831-6-7   Printed in Canada.

Expo 2004 is a book companion to The EXPO, a festival of cartoonists and comics publishers held annually in Bethesda, Maryland.

All proceeds from the book you now hold in your hands benefit the Comic Book Legal Defense Fund and help protect free expression in comics.

Turn to the final pages of this book for more information on the Expo and the Comic Book Legal Defense Fund.

War is the engine of history. Old as humankind itself, war has pushed forward the political, economic, and social systems that define us. Terrible, sometimes necessary, and always costly, war has proved itself, for better or worse, a constant in human history.

We study war using cold statistics, but we understand it with stories. This book is a collection of stories by 30 cartoonists from across the globe, who are using comics to explore the complexities of war.

In these pages you will see a variety of perspectives, from the personal to the polemical, from the historical to the allegorical. You will meet survivors and heroes, victims and villains, enemies and allies. Beneath the various roles and political values in each of these pieces, you will encounter a fundamental drive to comprehend the realities and value of war.

This book is hardly the last word on this subject in comics or any other artform. But it is a solid representation of the questions and crises facing us as we adapt to being a culture in conflict. Its authors question, condemn, and lament the inevitability of war, while speaking proudly of the durability of the human spirit in the face of its challenges.

We invite you now you to join these storytellers as they engage you in a conversation on the question of war...

The Editors of SPX 2004

**The Comic Book Legal Defense Fund**

The Comic Book Legal Defense Fund is a non-profit organization defending the First Amendment rights of the comics community. Founded in 1986, the CBLDF'S guiding doms guaranteed by the First Amendment and enjoyed by film, literature, visual art and other media.

The CBLDF helps insure that comics will continue to grow and develop as a vehicle for art, for invention, and for diversity. Thanks to generous support from comics fans and professionals alike, the CBLDF has provided free legal advice and defense for dozens of comics creators, retailers, and librarians in cases involving parody, obscenity, free access, and more. For more information about the CBLDF, please visit

wwww.cbldf.org or call **1-800-99-CBLDF**

## Your Correspondants...

*Building it Up Just to Tear it Down* / **Alex Lukas** / info@cantabpublishing.com ............ **1**

*Leaflet Drop* / **Drew Weing** / drew@drewweing.com ............................ **9**

*War Atrocity Love Song* / **Jamie Tanner** / jamietanner@gmail.com ................ **13**

*Dropping a Bomb* / **Justin Hall** / justin@allthumbspress.com .................... **21**

*April Fool's Tale* / **Jakob Klemencic** / jaka@pathfindermail.com ................ **25**

*Lost Letter* / **Scott White** / staticstudios@snotfair.com ...................... **32**

*Staying in There* / **Robert Bienvenu** / bienvenu@redcitycomics.com .............. **39**

*Blonds Have More Fun* / **Matt Dembicki** / m@waspcomics.com .................... **43**

*Untitled* / **Winston Rowntree** / chris_r41@hotmail.com ........................ **51**

*Pray* / **Federico Reggiani** & **Angel Mosquito** / moscu9@yahoo.com.ar .......... **63**

*White Death* / **Kurt A. Belcher** & **Philipp S. Neundorf** / chucklescat@hotmail.com ........ **70**

*Victory* / **Vladan Nikolic** / nvla@ptt.yu .................................... **76**

*The Holy Kingdom* / **Bruce Mutard** / filmnut66@yahoo.com ...................... **82**

*Ecaep* / **Diana Yee** / newstreamer@hotmail.com ................................ **94**

*The Sweet War* / **B. Vranken** / branken@zeelandnet.nl ........................ **103**

*Flight* / **Joey Weiser** / jweise20@student.scad.edu .......................... **115**

*FRatty: The Embittered Vietnam Vet* / **Bart Johnson** / aardbart@mindspring.com ........ **121**

*Toast* / **Ben Towle** / ben@teachingcomics.org ................................ **126**

*Come Back, Colin Powell* / **Jeff Smith** ...................................... **131**

*War is Just a Card Game..* / **Corinne Mucha** / maidenhousefly@hotmail.com ........ **135**

*Saturday Morning Showdown* / **J. Chris Campbell** / me@jchriscampbell.com ........ **139**

*Fuck the Troops* / **Megan Kelso** & **Ron Rege** / megan@girlhero.com ............ **150**

*U.S.A. War™ Instruction Manual* / **Lonnie Allen** / lonnie@dadagraphics.com ...... **151**

*Leaders & Followers* / **Charles Riffenburg IV** / chuck@grabbagcomics.com ........ **158**

*Underground: Maquis* / **Matt Bellisle** / gravitydsn@new.rr.com ................ **166**

*Good God, Y'all* / **Weatherwise** / weatherwise@borealism.com .................. **174**

*A Brief History of War* / **Michael Narren** / PFilm@comcast.net ................ **181**

**BUILDING IT UP JUST TO TEAR IT DOWN**

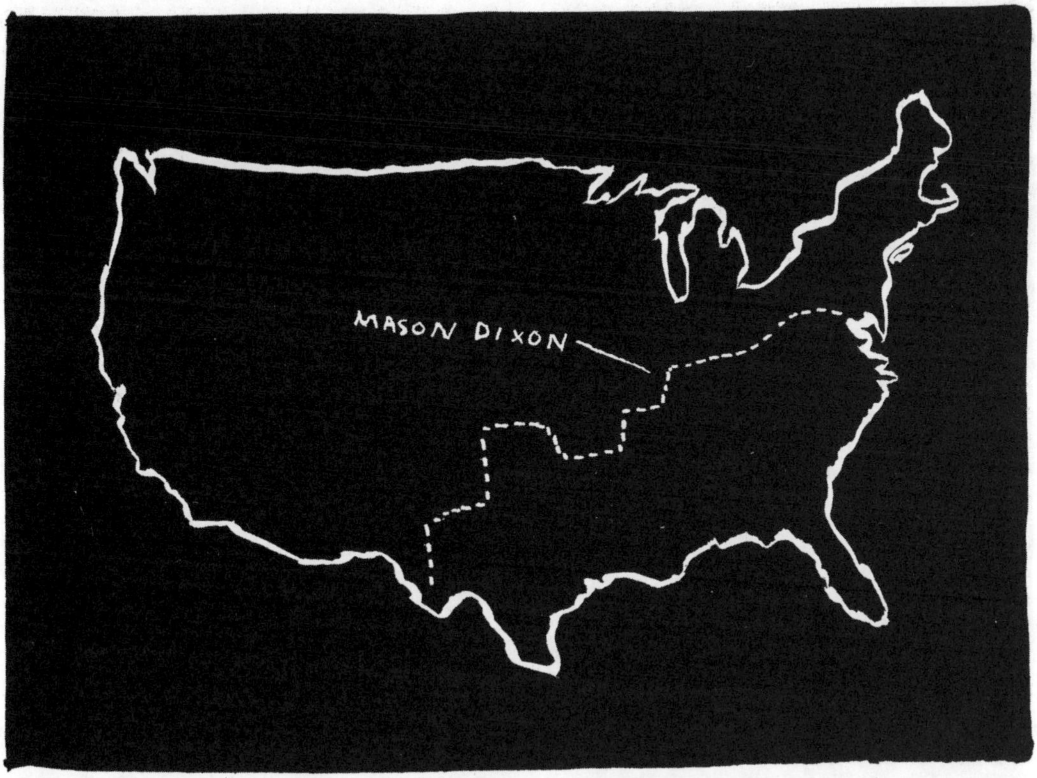

BASED ON THE 1864 PHOTOGRAPH BY ANDREW J. RUSSELL ENTITLED "METHOD OF DESTROYING RAILROAD TIES AND RAILS"

I lost my voice and learned to play. I still play those songs for my wife for anyone who will listen and the music always makes me think of birds.

# APRIL FOOL'S TALE

J.K. 2004

This guy was the absolute star of "Elisa". Never without a cue.

People said he even took it with him to the army medical exams... Yes, he was always different from the rest of us with our humdrum excuses: faking bad eyesight or hearing, eating raw potatoes...

Few of us were lucky. He was no exception there.

Later he said he might even have stayed if there had been a pool table in the barracks. Well, he liked to bullshit...

Anyway, he soon resorted to the usual method used when you were ready to get out: you went into a toilet stall without locking it and made some superficial slits in your wrist...

Lots of blood, little damage, much effect.

. . .

He was back at "Elisa" within three weeks or so.

He was as brilliant as ever... He started behaving a bit strange, though... Some suspected he was afraid the army might have spies at "Elisa".

Still, life was more or less normal for him and even the fact that it was 199? didn't seem to matter.

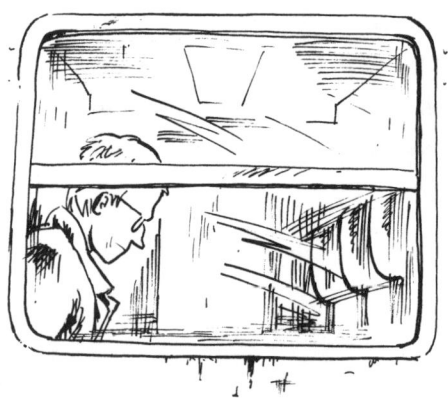

Then he was called up suddenly.

Apparently, that April somebody at the army HQ took the list of all the soldiers released after a suicide attempt... In the operation called "April Fools" they were sent to a shooting range where they worked indicating the hits on targets...

Some sort of a test. Lots of suicide opportunities...

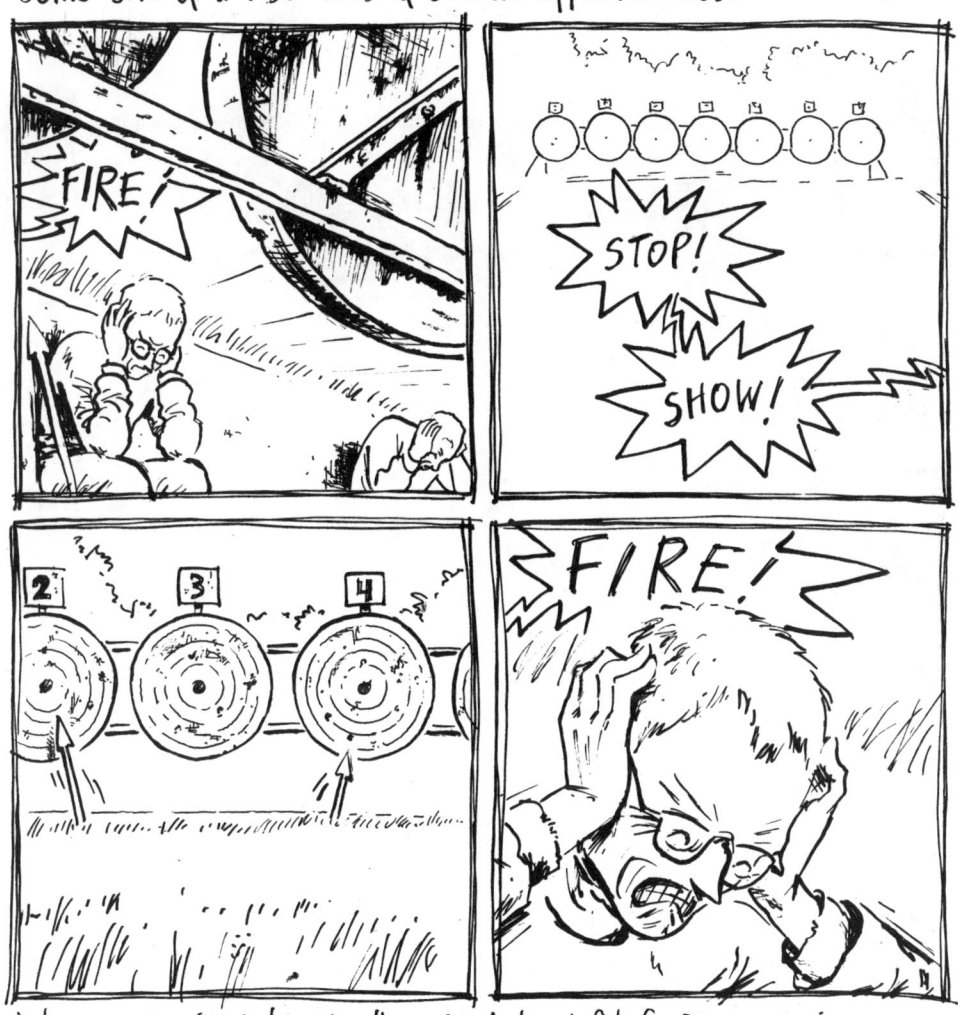

Whoever survived two months was declared fit for army service...

... And sent to the front. No weapon. They had to do chores like peeling potatoes, doing laundry and scrubbing the floor of a barracks where soldiers were spending time between two attacks. They would probably have lots of fun with someone accused of trying to get out of military service...

He never talked about it much when he came back.

...

That was about five weeks after the armistice.

Hello.

His only source of income was gone... his hands were shaking too much and no amount of alcohol would calm them down... He probably wouldn't have cared about the headaches and the insomnia if only his hands have been OK...

So... he decided to wrap it up... Anyway, how about this one?

"Who? That one? The owner's brother-in-law or something."

"A war hero."

# Blonds Have More Fun

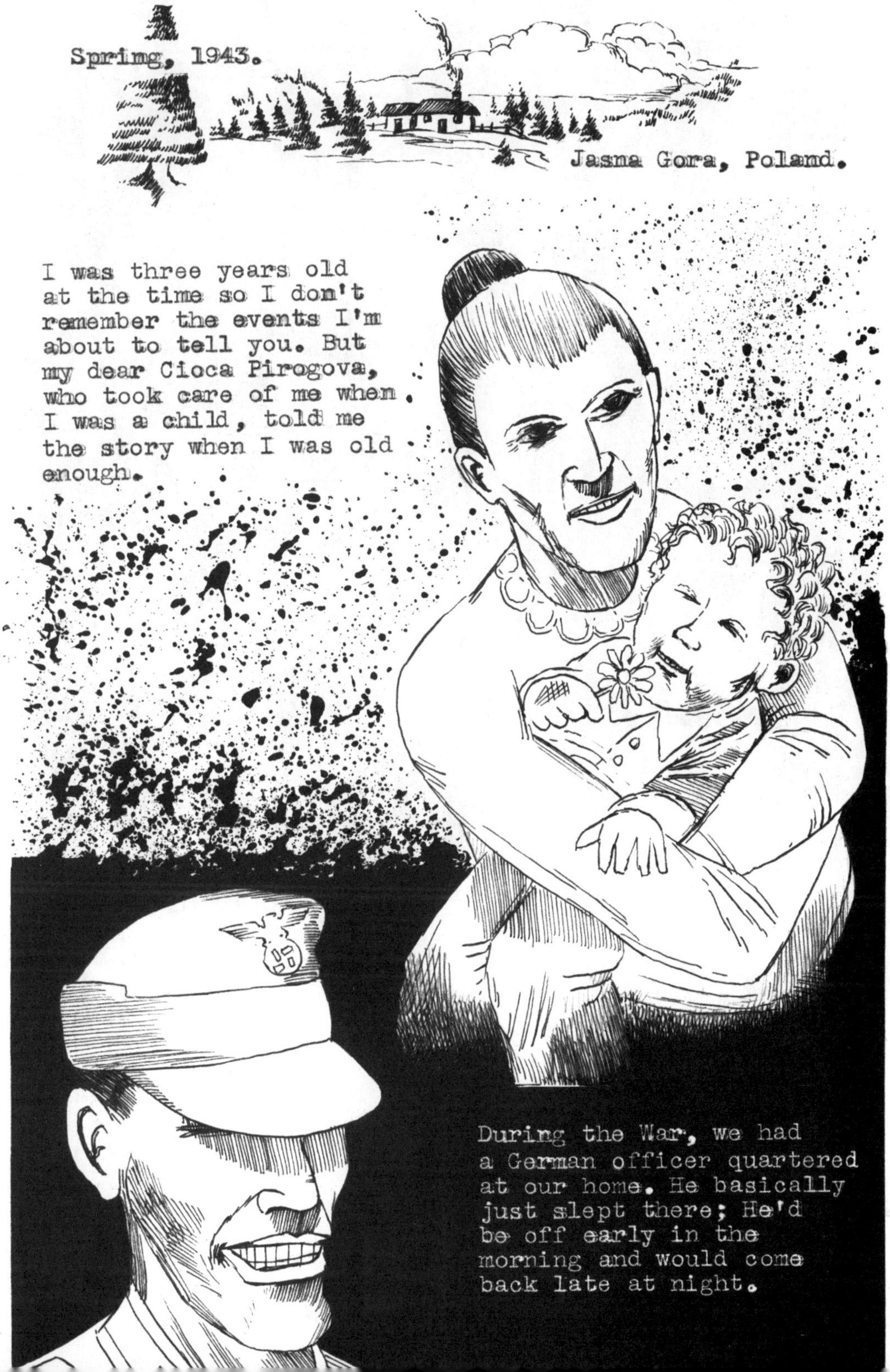

Spring, 1943.

Jasna Gora, Poland.

I was three years old at the time so I don't remember the events I'm about to tell you. But my dear Cioca Pirogova, who took care of me when I was a child, told me the story when I was old enough.

During the War, we had a German officer quartered at our home. He basically just slept there; He'd be off early in the morning and would come back late at night.

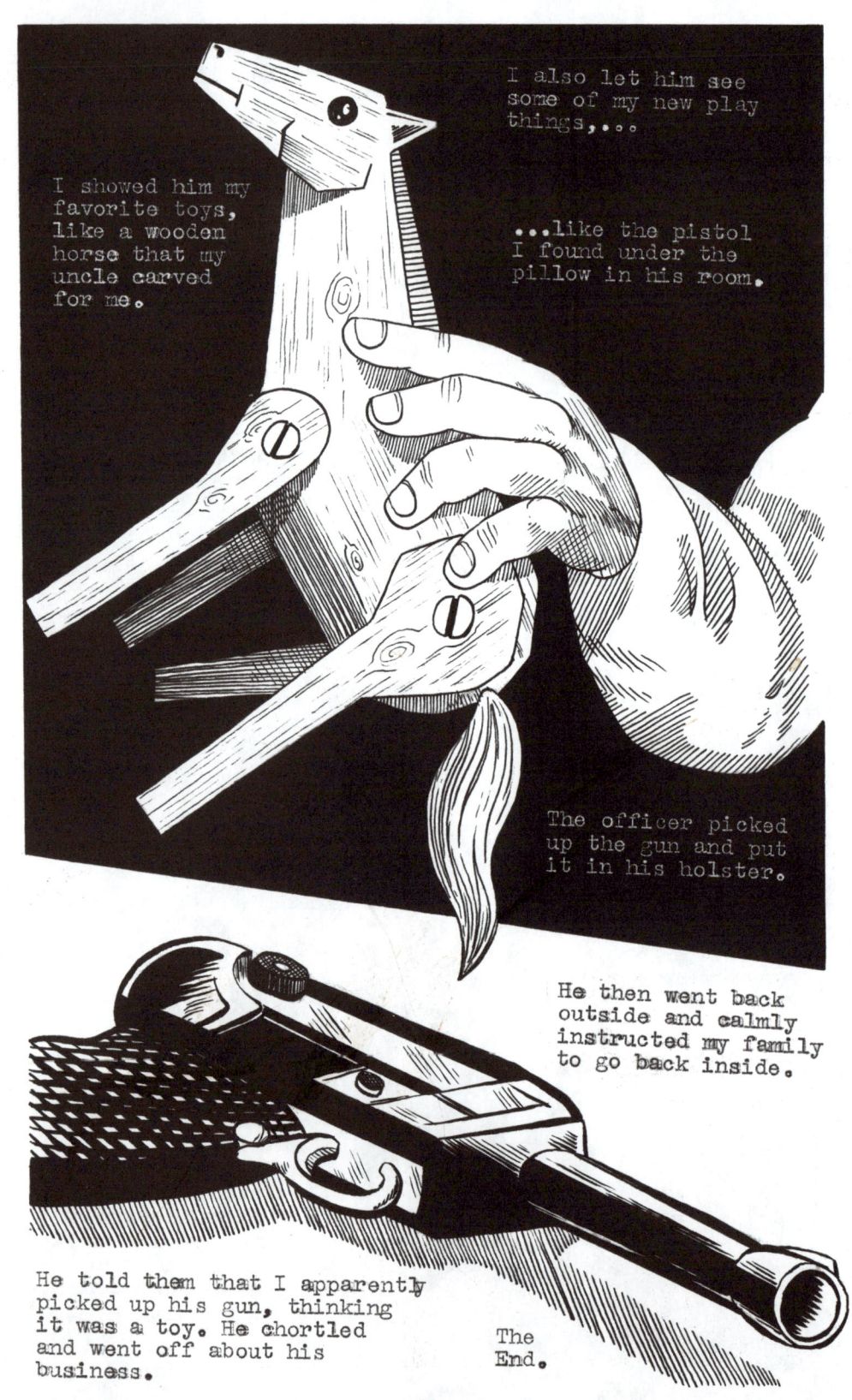

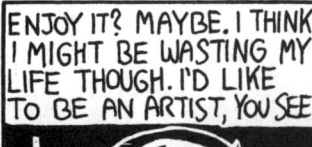

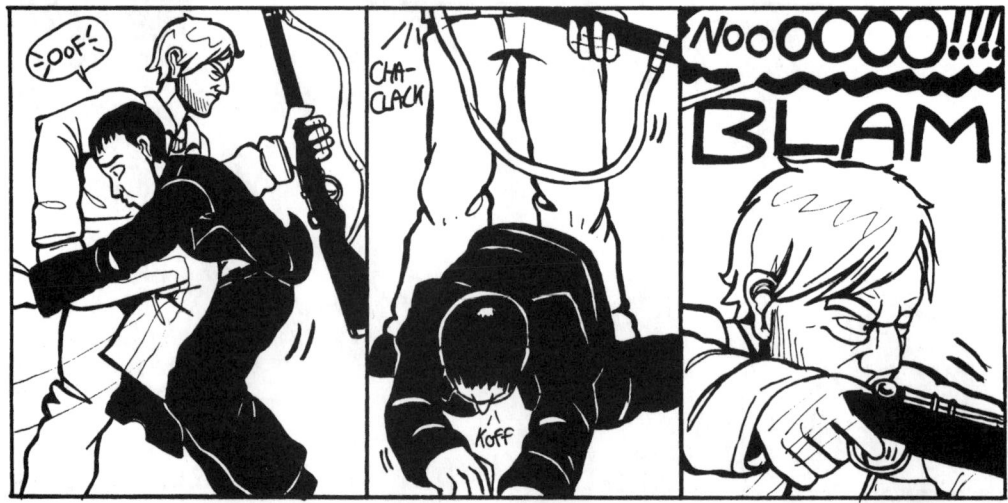

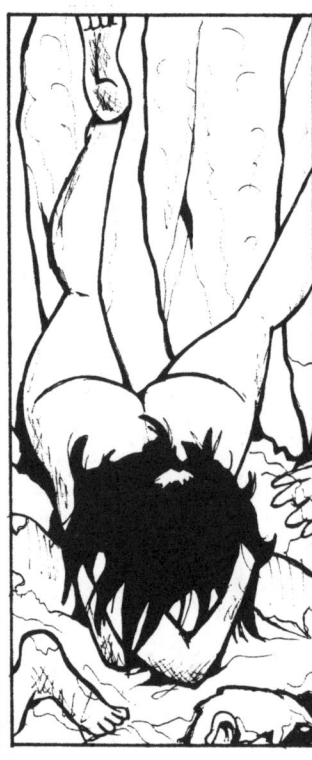

On September 29th & 30th, 1941, 33,771 Jews were murdered in the Babi Yar Ravine, Ukraine.

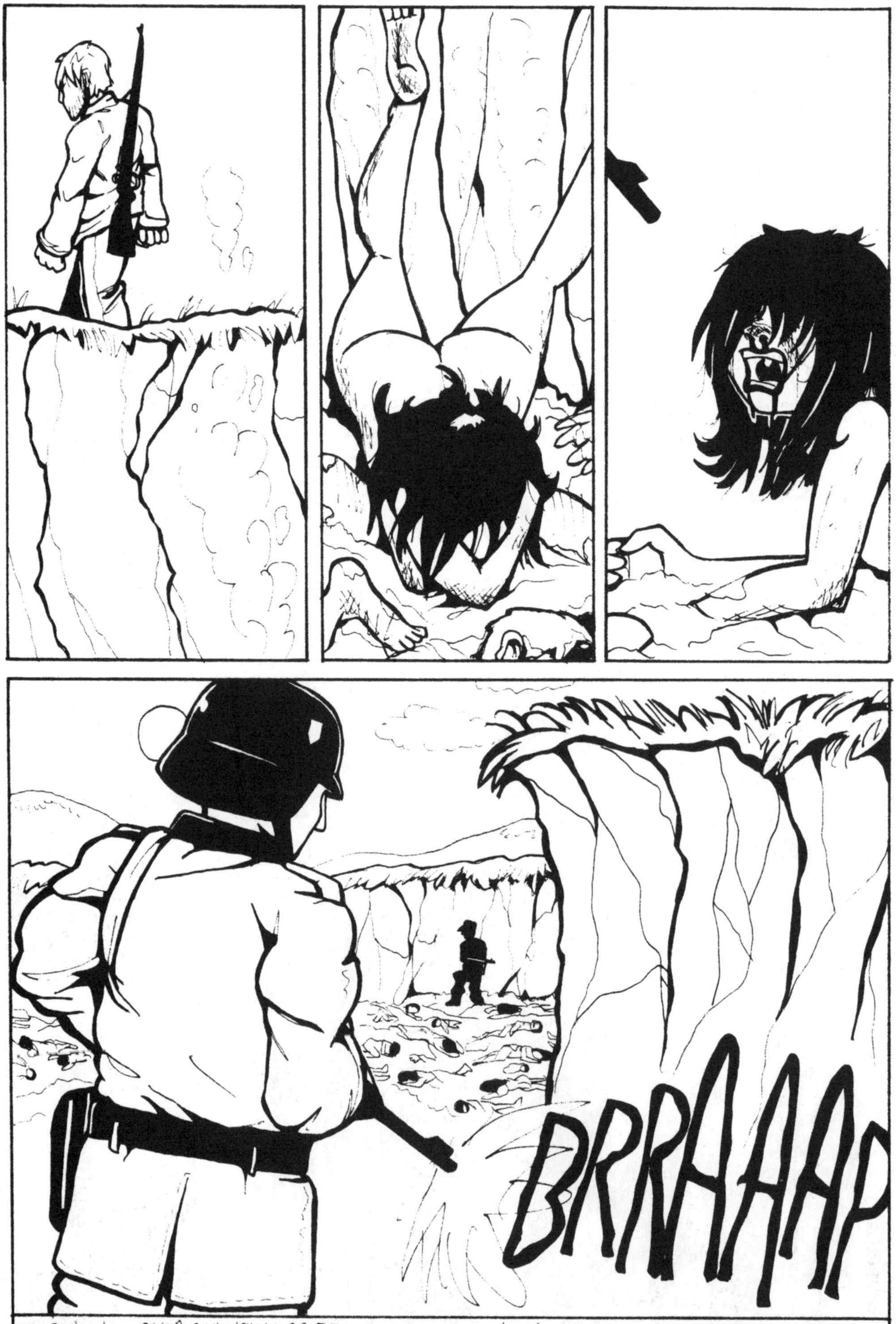

F. EDERICO REGGIANI + ANGEL MOSQUITO + 2004 - PLEASE CHECK WWW.LAPRODUCTORA.COM.AR. ARGENTINA

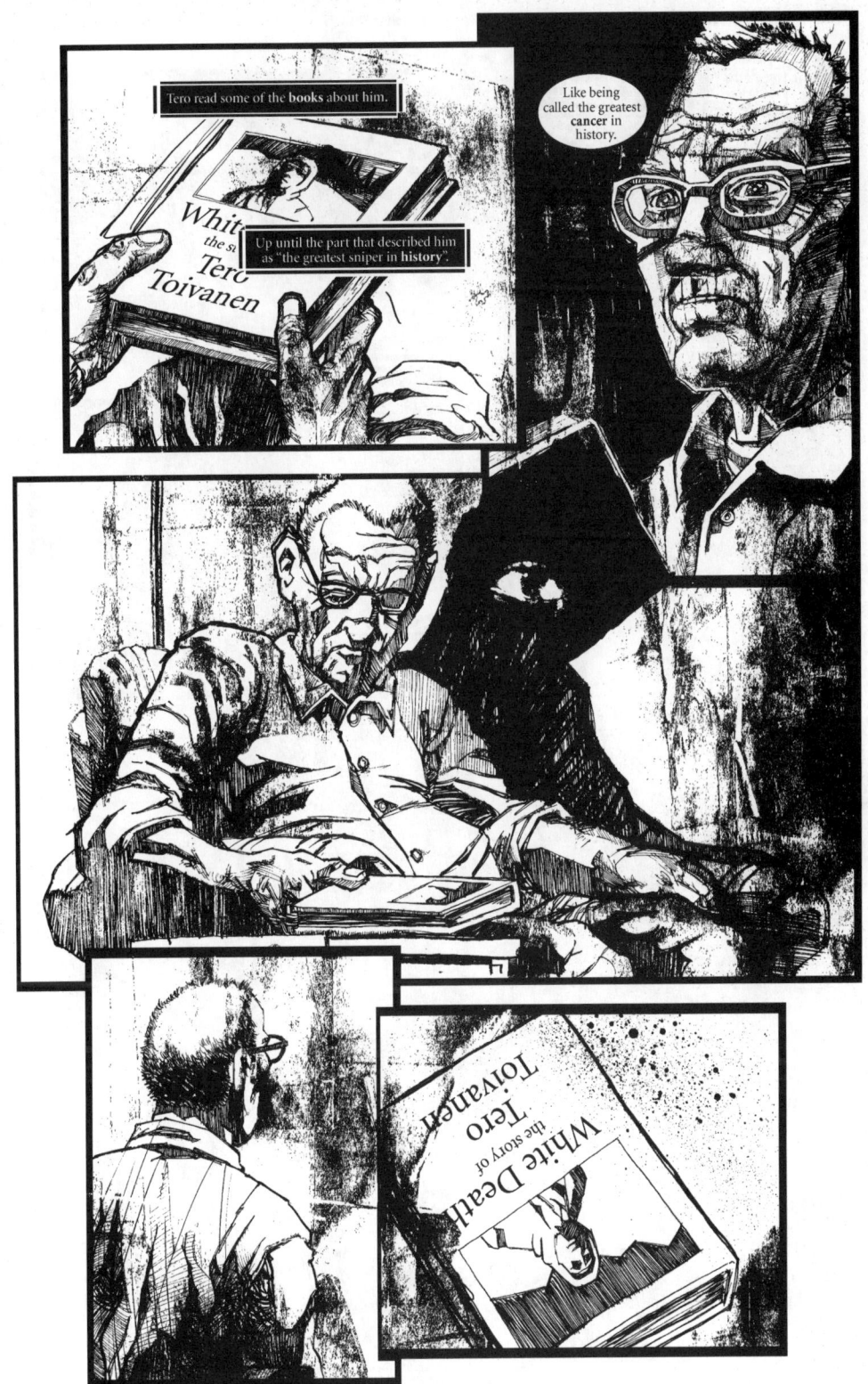

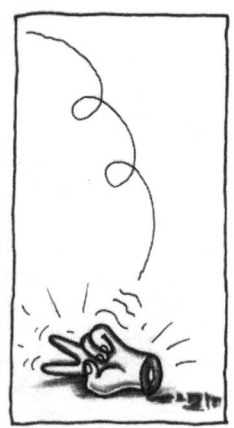

# VICTORY

BY: VLADAN NIKOLIĆ

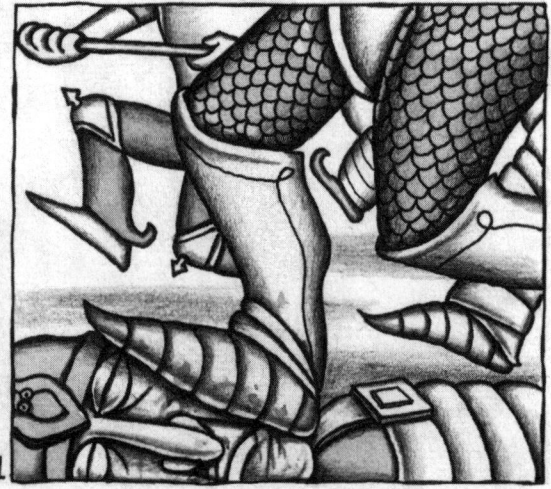

After Goya: Duelo a Garrotazos (Duel with clubs) 1820-24.

* Truncated version of Pope Urban II speech of 1095, from Durant, Age of Faith, p. 587, NY 1950.

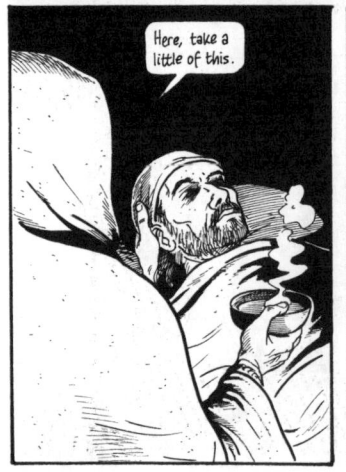

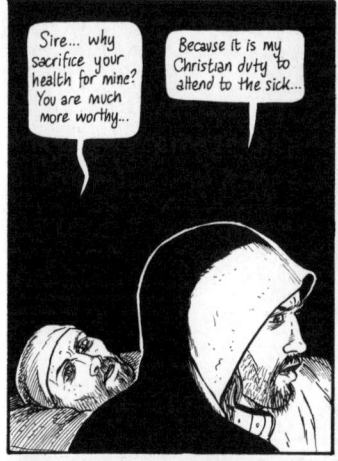

* Feast that concludes Ramadan.    * Sura 9.

* Matt 15:14

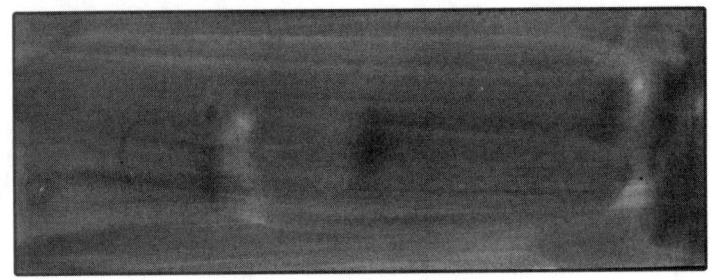

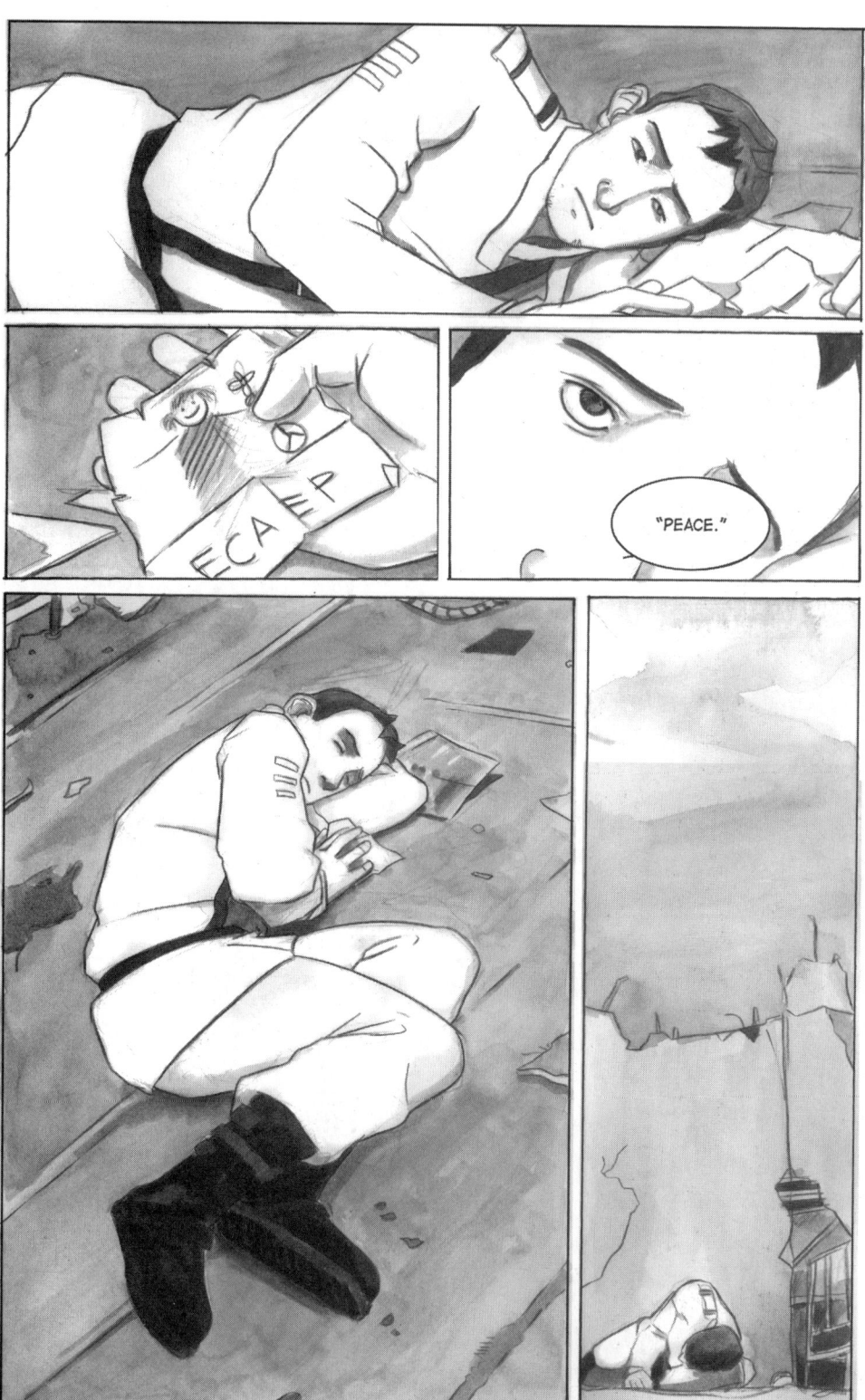

Some of us managed to escape however; they returned later to lay our heads by the roadside for the undertaker to collect.

The town was never erected again and it took the few survivors years to get over the massacre.

"WE LIKE TO KEEP THINGS PLEASANT AROUND HERE..."

Adults prefer to stay silent and stick to growing sugar-beets.

9.

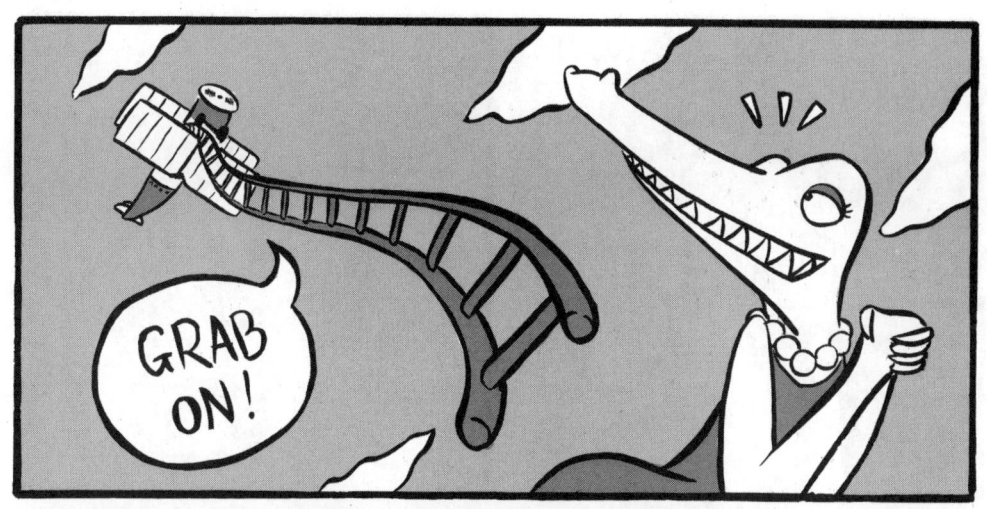

# COME BACK, COLIN POWELL!

I DON'T KNOW WHAT TO THINK ANYMORE! THE INTERNET IS **FULL** OF CONSPIRACY THEORIES -- GLOBAL EMPIRES, PIPELINES, A JEWISH CONSPIRACY -- A **SAUDI PRINCE** CONSPIRACY!

BUT WE NEED **SOME** KIND OF A THEORY TO EXPLAIN WHAT OUR GOVERNMENT IS DOING OR ELSE IT MAKES NO SENSE!

'I MEAN, FIRST WE SAY IRAQ HAS NUKES, THEN WE FIND OUT THEY DON'T HAVE NUKES... NORTH KOREA **DOES** HAVE NUKES, AND NOW WE'RE CLAIMING **IRAN** HAS THEM! MEANWHILE, WE ARE LETTING OSAMA BIN LADEN RUN WILD!'

MAYBE IT'S TRUE! MAYBE WE REALLY **ARE** AFTER THE OIL!

**OOOh!** WOULDN'T IT BE **MADDENING** IF THAT WERE TRUE?!

THERE **IS** ONE RAY OF HOPE -- THE **U.N.** IS LEADING THE EFFORT IN IRAN INSTEAD OF US. WE CAN TRUST THE **UNITED NATIONS** NOT TO GO ALONG WITH ANY SECRET PLAN TO TAKE OVER THE WORLD, CAN'T WE?

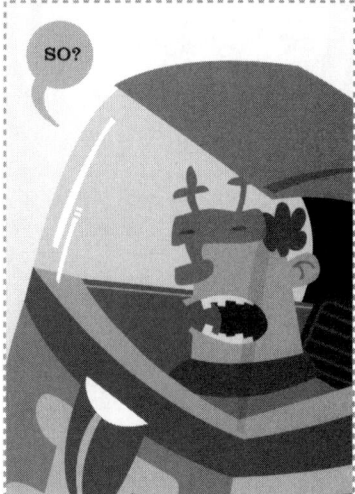

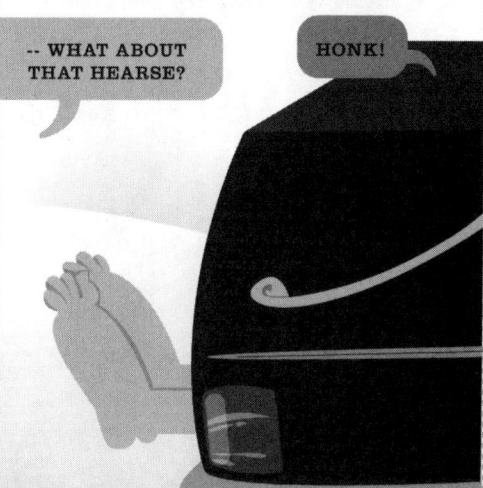

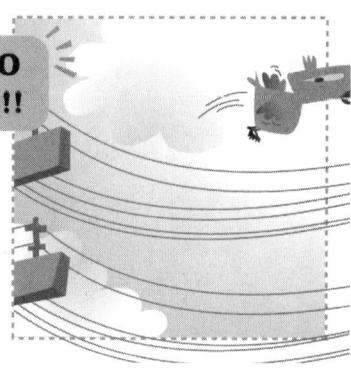

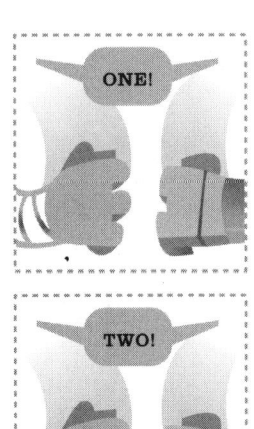
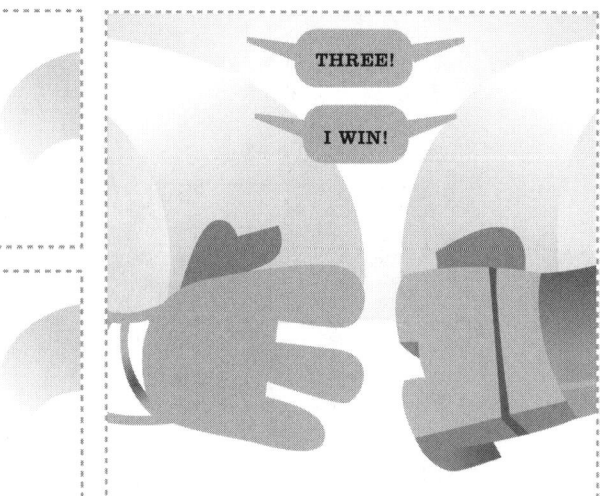

Megan Kelso & Ron Regé

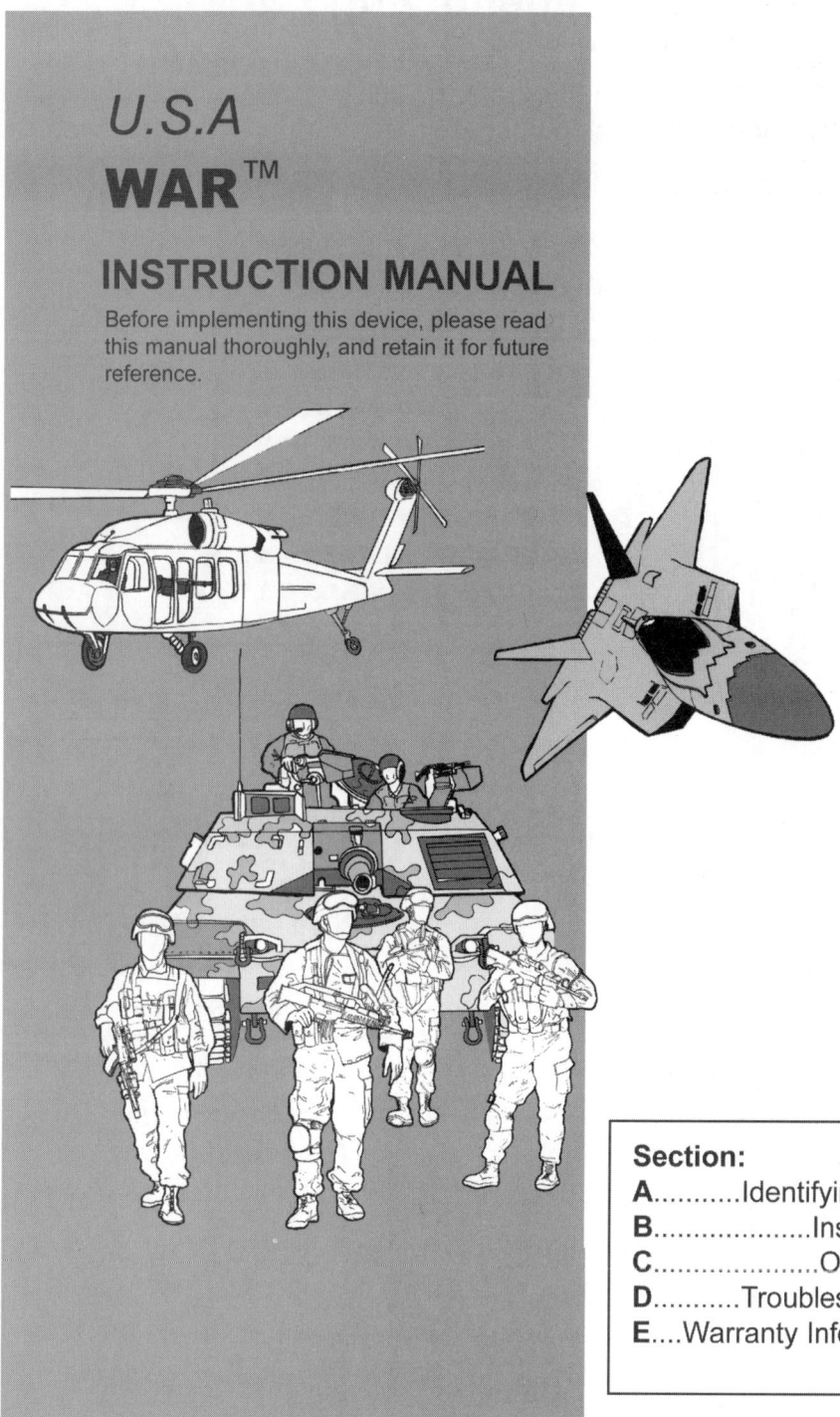

# U.S.A
# WAR™

## INSTRUCTION MANUAL

Before implementing this device, please read this manual thoroughly, and retain it for future reference.

**Section:**
A...........Identifying Parts
B....................Installation
C.....................Operation
D...........Troubleshooting
E....Warranty Information

Lonnie Allen

# Section A: Identifying Parts

Congratulations U.S. taxpayer on your purchase of U.S.A War™, the world's state of the art military offensive featuring new phrases, surgical precision, incredibly exciting graphics and great global domination.

Before you begin, take the time to identify the parts involved in U.S.A War™.

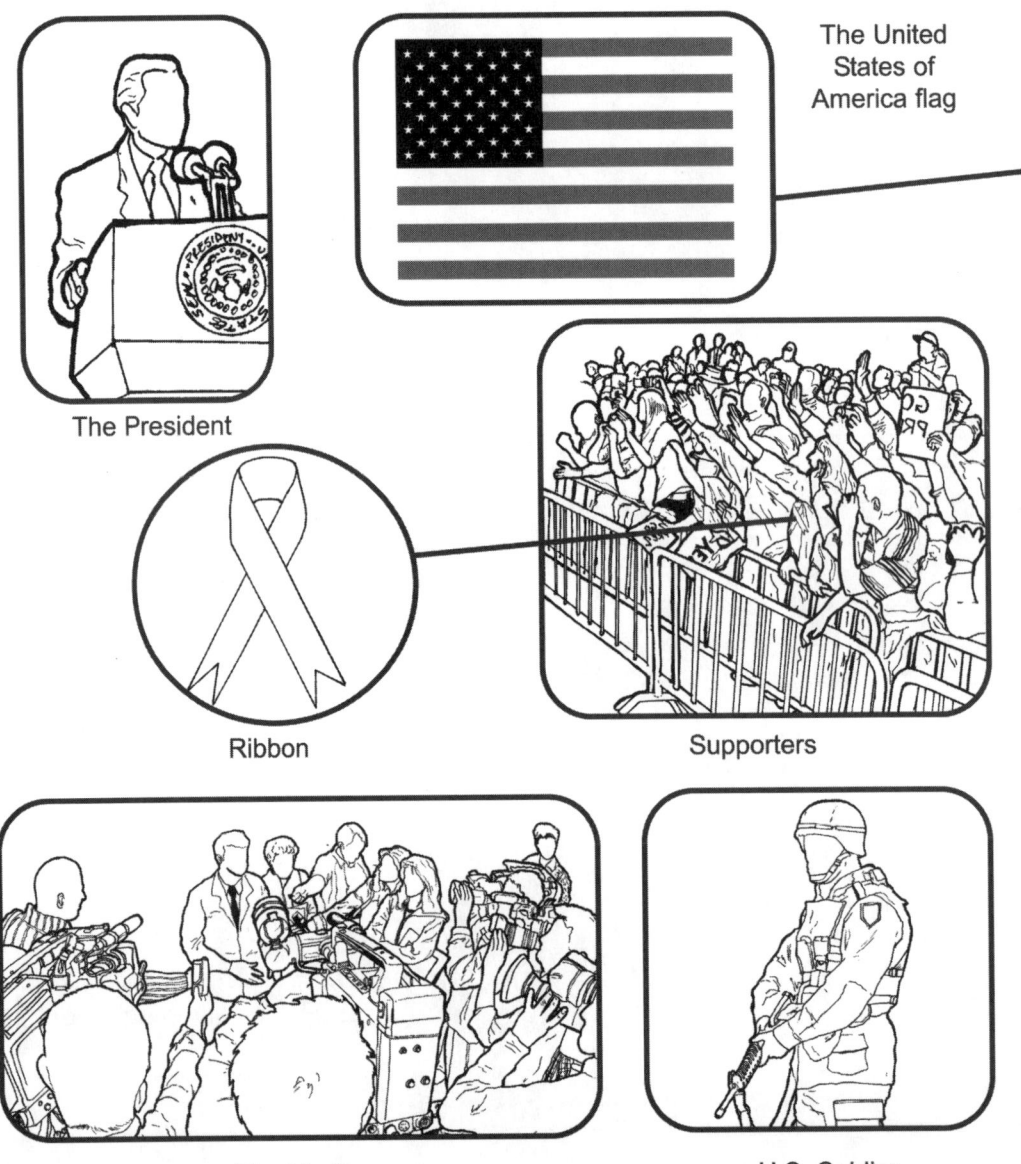

The President

The United States of America flag

Ribbon

Supporters

The Media

U.S. Soldier

The Enemy

Protesters
Note: To be allowed only in Free Speech Zones

Congress

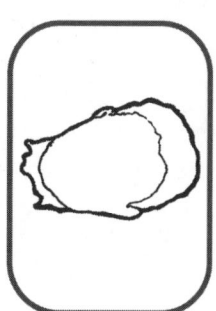

Head

Oil

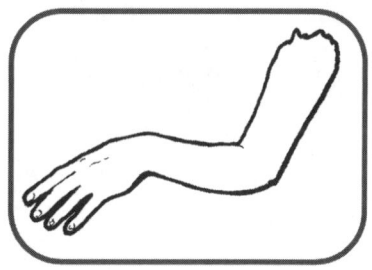

Arm

Money

Ballot Box

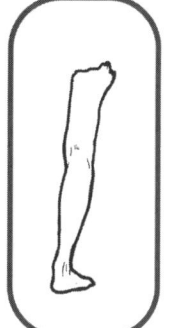

Leg

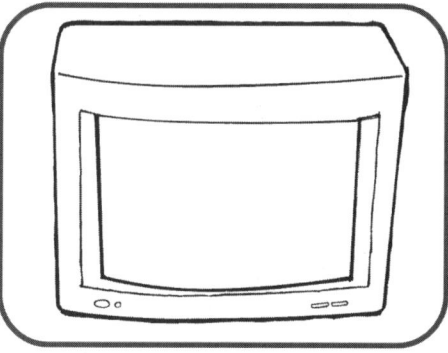

Television or T.V. for short

U.S. Taxpayer

# Section B: Installation

U.S.A War™ installation is easier than ever! For the most part, it's self-installing! Here are some steps, however, to help ensure a smooth installation:

Step 1: Vote for a president and/or other politician(s), or don't; one gets elected either way.

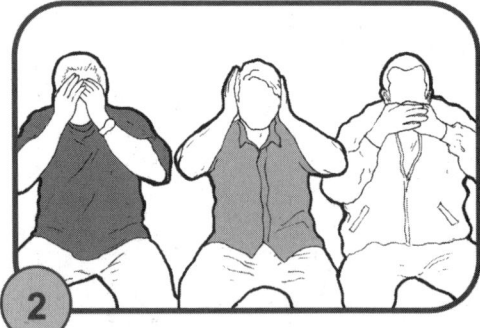

Step 2: Avoid voicing, seeing, and hearing any critical concerns about U.S.A War™.

Step 3: Adorn your house and/or your body with ribbons and flags to demonstrate your patriotism!

Step 4: Contribute your part to xenophobia and/or overall paranoia.

Step 5: Watch an abundance of vapid television.

Step 6: Pay your taxes on time.

# Section C: Operation

With U.S.A War™ properly installed, you may now begin to use it's many wonderful features. This newest model has all the features of previous versions as well as new ones.

Feel superior for being part of a nation bringing wealth and democracy to the world.

Try buying an SUV and/or some other gas inefficient vehicle.

You can now mock, maim, and/or deride an enemy race, religion, and/or nationality

Warning: Do not practice any other form of free speech.

Invest in oil companies and make money before the bottom falls out.

Watch exciting reality-show action on the daily news.

# Section D: Troubleshooting

Before trying to contact technical support, try these simple solutions to some problems you may experience.

## Problem            Solution

Unemployment occurs to you during the war.

Join the military; you'll visit exciting locations, kill without going to jail, and get paid.

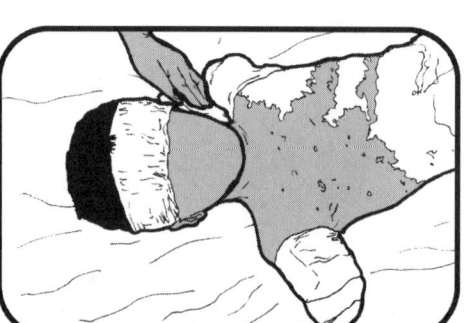

Troubling images appear on the television and/or in the newspaper.

Go out shopping.

You develop a profound feeling that we are not doing the right thing.

Go out shopping.

# Section E: Warranty Information

ANY APPLICABLE IMPLIED WARRANTIES ARE HEREBY LIMITED IN DURATION TO THE WARRANTY PERIODS DESCRIBED ABOVE (ONE PRESIDENTIAL TERM OR TWO, AS APPLICABLE). IN NO EVENT SHALL THE U.S. GOVERNMENT BE LIABLE FOR CONSEQUENTIAL OR INCIDENTAL DEATH RESULTING FROM THE BREACH OR AN IMPLIED OR EXPRESSED WARRANTIES. SOME COUNTRIES DO NOT ALLOW LIMITATIONS ON HOW LONG AN IMPLIED WARRANTY LASTS OR EXCLUSIONS OF CONSEQUENTIAL OR INCIDENTAL DEATH, SO THE ABOVE LIMITATIONS MAY NOT APPLY TO YOU.

**WARNING**

TO PREVENT RIOTS, OR SHOCK HAZARD DO NOT EXPOSE TO CRITICAL THINKING.

**CAUTION**

THIS DEVICE DOES NOT COMPLY WITH GENEVA CONVENTION OR SOME CONSTITUTIONAL LAWS. OPERATION IS SUBJECT TO THE TWO CONDITIONS: (1) THIS DEVICE MAY CAUSE HARMFUL INTERFERENCE, AND (2) THIS DEVICE MUST NOT ACCEPT ANY INTERFERENCE RECEIVED, INCLUDING INTERFERENCE THAT MAY CAUSE UNDESIRED OPERATION OF NOT OBTAINING OUR GOD GIVEN RIGHT TO A WHOLE BUNCH OF STUFF WE WANT BECAUSE WE'RE AMERICANS GODDAMMIT.

For Technical assistance visit our website: **www.usa.gov** or Call us at **1-800-FED-INFO** that's **1-800-333-4636**

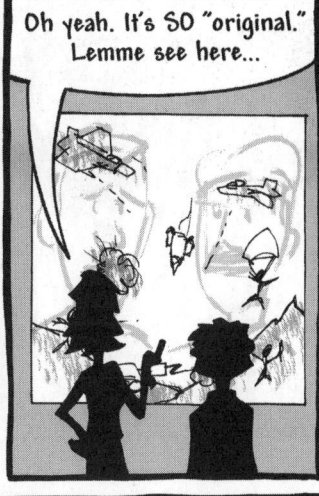

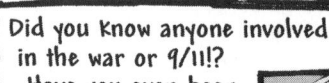

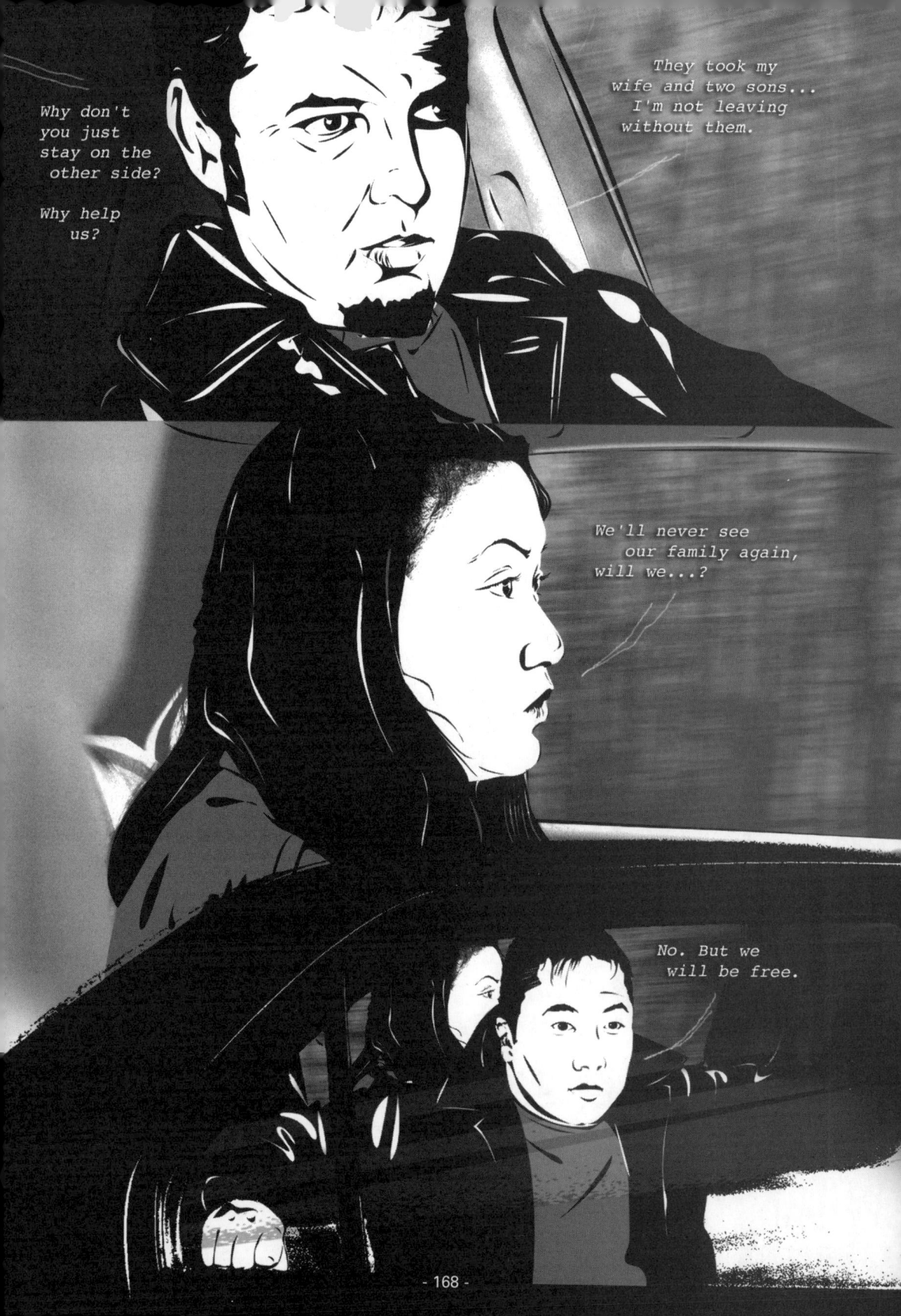

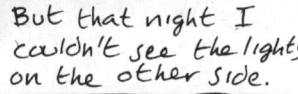

Copied from Colville, Alex. "Infantry, near Nijmegen". Canadian War Museum.

## SPX 2004

The EXPO is a non-profit organization with the primary purpose of promoting comics, animation, cartooning and related popular art forms through the presentation of conventions and events that celebrate the historic and ongoing contribution of those media to art and culture. The EXPO seeks to accomplish its purpose by providing a forum for people interested in exhibiting and admiring comics, animation, cartooning and related art forms through conventions and professional activities, and by awarding the Ignatz Awards annually to recognize outstanding talent and ability among creators. For more information about the EXPO, please visit www.spxpo.com.

## The 2004 SPX Steering Committee

Executive Director: Steve Conley

Executive Committee: Greg Bennett, Greg McElhatton, Michael Zarlenga

Steering Committee: Jeff Alexander, Warren Bernard, Charles Brownstein, Karon Flage, John Gallagher, Cary Gordon, Elizabeth Gordon, Rich Henn, Chris Pitzer, Joel Pollack, Michael Thomas

Art: Joel Priddy | © King Features Syndicate

**Support the War Effort.** Purchase one of these fine documents from www.cbldf.org.

**Posters**

The 2004 SPX Poster. Art by Peter Kuper. ...$10 ...$15 signed

The 2003 SPX Poster. Art by Frank Cammuso. $10 ...$15 signed

The 2002 SPX Poster. Art by Jason Little. ...$10 ...$15 signed

The 2001 SPX Poster. Art by Nick Bertozzi. ...$10 ...$20 signed

**Books**

The 2004 SPX War-themed Anthology. ...$9.95

The 2003 SPX Travel-themed Anthology. ...$9.95

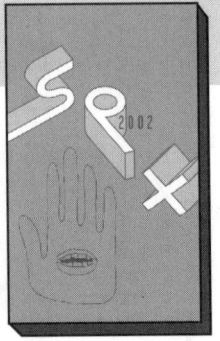

The 2002 SPX Biography-themed Anthology. ...$9.95

The 2001 SPX Anthology. ...$15 (limited quantities)

**Support the War Effort.** Purchase one of these fine documents from www.cbldf.org.